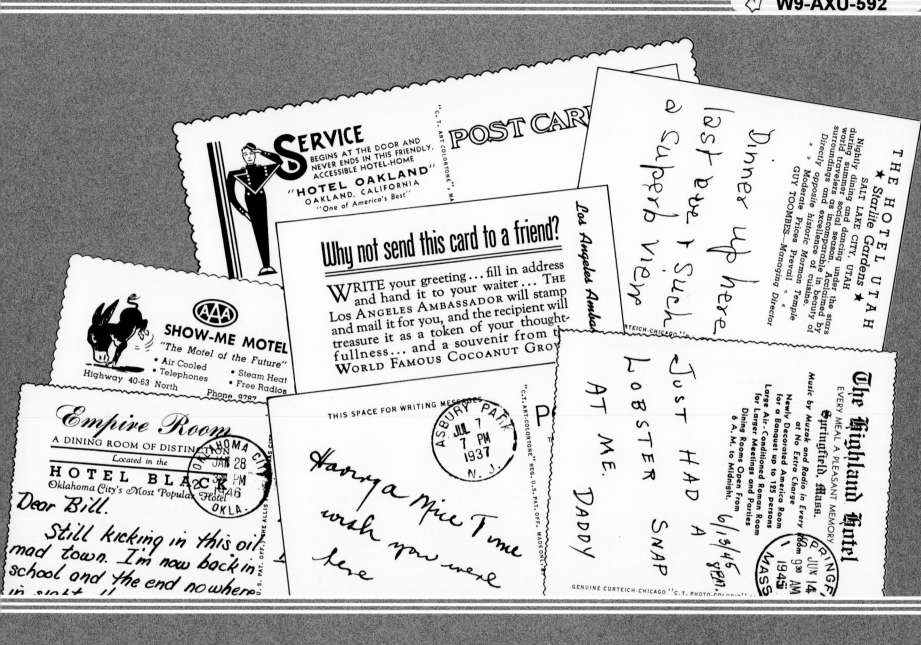

Grand View-Ship Hotel on Lincoln Highway, U. S. 30

SEE 3 STATES and 7 COUNTIES

VISITORS WELCOME
FREE TELESCOPE

3A-H422

17 Miles West of Bedford, Pa., 80 Miles East of Pittsburgh, Pa.

WISH YOU WERE HERE

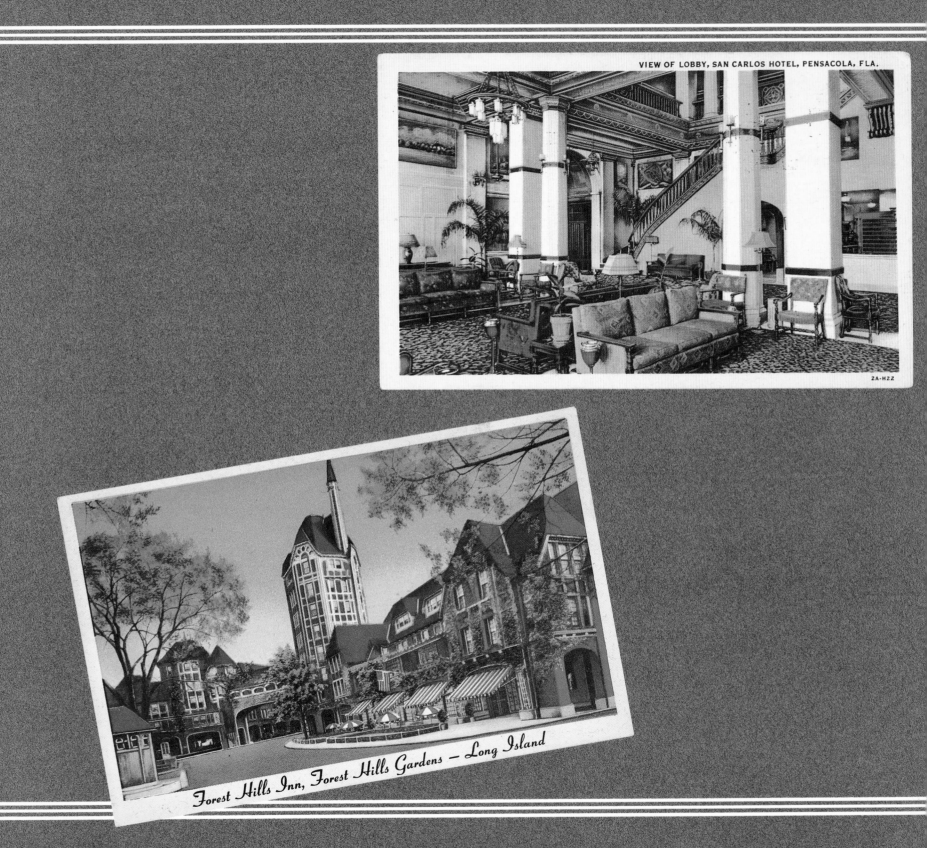

VIEW OF LOBBY, SAN CARLOS HOTEL, PENSACOLA, FLA.

2A-H2Z

Forest Hills Inn, Forest Hills Gardens — Long Island

WISH YOU WERE HERE

A Tour of
America's Great Hotels
During the Golden Age of
the Picture Post Card

POST CARD

THIS SPACE FOR ADDRESS ONLY

AUG 9
1 30 PM
19 34

YOSEMITE 1¢
U.S. POSTAGE

by Barry Zaid

CROWN PUBLISHERS, INC.
NEW YORK

Rest Rooms - **WIGWAM VILLAGE No. 1** - *Eat Shoppe*
U. S. 31E and 68 — 18 Miles East of Mammoth Cave —
31 Miles South of Lincoln's Birthplace

· **INSULATED INDIAN WIGWAMS** ·
Each with complete Bath, Hot and Cold Water,
Inner Spring Mattresses, and Solid Hickory Furniture
·
Always Open   **GAS and OIL**
Wigwams Built and Patented by
F. A. REDFORD, Prop.

WIGWAM VILLAGE No. 1

3 MILES EAST OF HORSE CAVE, KY., ON 31-E

6A-H184

WISH YOU WERE HERE

Published by Crown Publishers, Inc.,
201 East 50th Street, New York, New York 10022.
Member of the Crown Publishing Group.

Book design by Barry Zaid.

CROWN is a trademark of Crown Publishers, Inc.

Manufactured in Japan.

Library of Congress Cataloging-in-Publication Data.

Zaid, Barry.
Wish you were here: a tour of America's great hotels during the golden
age of the picture post card/Barry Zaid.
1. Postcards—United States. 2. Hotels, taverns, etc., in art. 3. Hotels,
taverns, etc.—United States—Pictorial works. 4. Zaid, Barry—Art
collections. 5. Postcards—Private collections.
I. Title.
NC1878.7.U6Z35 1990   90-1922
741.6'83'0973074—dc20
ISBN 0-517-58009-8
10 9 8 7 6 5 4 3 2 1
First Edition

POST CARD

PLACE
ONE CENT
STAMP
HERE

To my mother, whose albums
have been such a source of
inspiration.
And to Bob Carlson, for his
constant encouragement.

INTRODUCTION ▪ 6

CURT TEICH & COMPANY ▪ 8

CABINS, COURTS, AND COTTAGES ▪ 10

INNS ▪ 16

LODGES ▪ 23

THE GREAT RESORTS ▪ 28

CITY HOTELS ▪ 36

GRAND HOTELS ▪ 52

SOUTHWEST STYLE ▪ 56

FLORIDA, LAND OF SUNSHINE ▪ 63

THE GRAND FOYER ▪ 75

DINNER, DRINKS, AND DANCING ▪ 83

ACKNOWLEDGMENTS ▪ 94

RESOURCES ▪ 95

CONTENTS

At a country auction outside my native Toronto many years ago I bid on an old wooden carpenter's toolbox, which I planned to use as a coffee table. When I got it home and opened it up it turned out to contain some unexpected items: some short, wide neckties, a pair of checked linen knickers, and a rather beat-up imitation leather album half-full of old post cards. I was never able to discern any connection between the various cards in the collection, but as a graphic designer I found the different printing methods and styles fascinating. They piqued my curiosity and I began looking for more old cards. I subsequently spent a few years in England, where my collection grew to include some extravagant turn-of-the-century cards printed in twelve to fifteen colors, heavily embossed and embellished with metallic and opalescent colors. Some of these influenced my work greatly, and one of them, a picture of a girl relaxing in a hammock, beautifully printed by the British firm of Raphael Tuck and Sons, became the basis of a billboard I designed in the seventies for 7-Up.

Among the cards in that original album, though, were several more modest ones, printed on card stock embossed with a linen-like finish and depicting various buildings and tourist sites. Although I was primarily focusing on the fancier European cards, I kept noticing these American cards, which reminded me of those I remembered seeing at the general store near the summer cottage on Lake Simcoe, Ontario, that my family rented when I was young. Now I often saw such cards in the ten-for-a-dollar box of dealers' less desirable cards at antique and paper collectible shows, and gradually I began to look for them rather than the more collectible (and by then considerably more expensive) European cards.

To me there was something magical about those linen cards. The skyscrapers and monuments and bridges and beaches seemed so perfect. And those skies! The most gorgeous robin's-egg blues gently fading into pale peach tinged with just a blush of coral, a few wisps of fluffy white clouds floating overhead; the perfect foil for the main subject of the card, be it a movie star's Hollywood mansion, a fabulous municipal fountain, a spectacular natural wonder...or a hotel.

I had not always separated my collection into categories. At first I kept them all in a shoe box and would occasionally flip through them. Then one winter evening I began to spread them out on the floor and sort them into piles of cards of similar types. I eventually came across some plastic sheets, each designed to hold and protect four cards. At first the categories were pretty general, but as I started to group them in the plastic sheets, certain cards seemed to want to go together. One of the biggest groupings was a thick pile of cards of hotels. There were big hotels and small hotels, hotels in the city and hotels in the country. There were some very grand hotels and a grouping of Western-looking hotels. Then there were cabins and places calling themselves "inns" and resort hotels and, of course, motels. There were some rarer cards showing interiors: foyers and ballrooms and cocktail bars and coffee shops, often displaying a dazzling mix of theatrical architectural and decorative styles.

I became a linen-card junkie. I sought out (and dragged my friends to) more and more antique and collectible shows. I began to fill album after album. I created gorgeous layouts featuring narrower and narrower categories: fountains with colored water, Niagara Falls illuminated, streamlined trains roaring through orange groves, phallic monuments.

INTRODUCTION

But it was the hotel cards that multiplied at the most alarming rate. I kept dreaming of doing a book on my collection. Perhaps I would write a mystery book...I would use the hotel cards as a background as the subject traveled across the country. But I was not a writer, and anyway, the thing that was really interesting was the hotels themselves. Why not just create an album showing the best of them? Hence, this book.

As I was working on the first dummy for the book I learned more about linen cards. Inspecting some cards with a magnifying glass, I became aware that they were printed not with just the usual four colors that printers normally use to simulate full color (magenta, cyan blue, yellow, and black), but that there was an additional darker blue, which accounted for the richness of the blue skies. One of the things that had always fascinated me about these cards was that even though they were photographic images, they were obviously hand colored, not simply taken from color photographs. Here was a synthesis of painting and photography resulting in a photographic look, with the clarity of color and detail that only an artist could create.

The cards served as building portraits, and they strived to show their subjects in the most flattering way. Each hotel stood majestically separate from other buildings or distracting elements. There were no telephone poles or wires scarring the skies. Flowers and trees were

LOBBY — THE ROOSEVELT — NEW YORK

always in full bloom, and shadows, if any, were a rich and lovely lavender. Interiors were free of distracting patrons. This was a world even better than reality.

Not only that, but this was a world frozen in time, a world that in many cases no longer exists. Many of the buildings on these pages have been so altered over the years that they bear little or no resemblance to what has been preserved on these cards. (Some have merely been modified to reflect more up-to-date tastes, and I have included a few sets of cards that demonstrate this before-and-after effect.) Some of the hotels, once grand, have fallen to become welfare hotels or have been knocked down altogether as neighborhoods changed. Still others, happily, have been rediscovered and restored to their original splendor.

But in the cards all the hotels are in their prime. This is a trip across America that we can still take. We can imagine that that is us sunning in front of the splendid Marlborough-Blenheim on Atlantic City's golden, sandy beach or strolling through the magnificent cactus gardens of Phoenix's Camelback Inn or enjoying the view of the mountains through the tall windows of the Prince of Wales Hotel in Canada's Waterton Lakes National Park. Isn't that our table in the tree-lined dining room, beside the gurgling brook that runs through the lodge in Brookdale, California? This is visual history, a record of the traveler's life of yesteryear.

8

While this book presents a variety of America's most interesting hotels, both large and small, it is also a tribute to a generation of largely anonymous commercial photographers and retouchers who inadvertently became America's national architectural portrait artists.

When I first started collecting linen cards I was not aware that most of them, and certainly the best of them, had been produced by one company, Curt Teich & Company, Inc., of Chicago. Teich's story is a classic tale of American success and tragedy. Born in 1877 in Germany, he studied the printing trade and moved to Chicago as a teenager. There he worked as a printer for two and a half years before starting his own company. Competition among printers was fierce, so in 1904 Curt Teich returned to Germany (which with England was in the forefront of printing technology) to study the latest in printing and lithographic processes. On his return to Chicago he developed a new process of printing post cards, combining black-and-white halftone plates and adding colors through lithography. Ultimately a number of skilled German artists joined his firm. Thinking his process too complicated to be imitated, Teich neglected to protect it by patent, and indeed other European printers did follow his methods. However, Teich held a competitive edge over imported competition because of his faster turnaround (sixty to ninety days versus six to twelve months for imported cards) and an import duty that protected his narrow profit margin. He managed to keep ahead of the competition by attracting talented technicians and by initiating two work shifts. The company continued to prosper throughout the depression and survived various ups and downs to become, by 1939, as his son Ralph described it, "the General Motors of the post card area throughout the world."

In response to the threat of World War II, Teich's three

CURT TEICH & COMPANY

oldest sons enlisted in the military. Tragically, his beloved third son, Lawrence, disappeared, presumably killed when the Japanese ship on which he was a prisoner was either torpedoed or bombed by American forces. Grief stricken, the elder Teich's health deteriorated and control of the company was handed over to his eldest son, Curt Jr., who lacked his father's experience. Business problems were compounded after the war by the company's failure to respond as quickly as its competitors to the development of true photographic color separation. Teich's "fake" color cards attracted fewer orders; it thus took longer to put together enough cards to fill the large multiple presses, and longer to fulfill the dwindling orders. Curt Teich & Company, once the home of forty presses and a thousand employees, was reduced to two presses run by seventy-eight men when it shut down in 1974. Fortunately, however, all correspondence, printing plates, photographs, and samples of fabric, carpeting, and linoleum used as artists' guides were given to the Lake County Museum, about forty miles northwest of Chicago, where it now forms the nucleus of the Curt Teich Postcard Archives.

Ever since I started collecting the Teich cards, I was curious about the steps involved in their actual production. According to Ralph Teich (Curt's youngest son), a traveling salesman for the company would take a black-and-white photograph of a hotel, and then would return to the hotel with the developed print to get approval and an initial order from the proprietor, making note of any objectionable items that were to be retouched out. Then, using a large card of numbered color swatches, the salesman would record the colors that matched each element of the building. The photograph would then go to Teich's art department, where desired changes were made: for example, if there was a hole in the hedges, an artist would make a duplicate print of the hedge and strip it in. Then clouds would be airbrushed in and five final prints would be made, one for each of the printing colors (magenta, yellow, black, cyan blue, and the special dark blue that Teich used to add richness to his skies). For each of the colors noted on the swatch card there was a formula indicating the percentage of each of the printing colors required to make that particular color. At one time there were 150 people working eight hours a day on this color-separating process alone. Finally a proof was pulled to show to the client. Any changes at this point would require a completely new set of plates, but it was important to please the client because all the profit depended upon subsequent reprintings. Ultimately, the card would become part of a larger printing plate that printed thirty-two cards at a time.

It is estimated that Curt Teich & Company printed some 400,000 different views of the United States, Canada, and overseas over a period of seventy-seven years.

Something that makes Teich cards particularly interesting and valuable from a historical point of view is that most of them bear a code that can be easily deciphered to reveal the date of production. The code begins with a single number followed by the letter A, B, or C, then a dash and an H and more numbers. An A indicates that the card was produced in the 1930s; a B, the 1940s; and a C, the 1950s. The preceding number is the year within that decade. Therefore, a card with the code 2A-H156 was produced in 1932. The second part of the code, starting with H, is the company's internal job number.

I have included several pairs of cards showing views of the same hotel or room a few years apart, before and after alterations or changes in decorating schemes. It is fascinating to compare the differences and to observe the changes in fashion. Colors considered the last word one year become tired and old-hat a few years later. Over the years much has been lost due to vagaries of fashion, but those hotels that, through the sheer excellence of their original design, careful maintenance, and the confidence of their management, plus a bit of luck concerning continuing popularity of their location, managed to resist change have ultimately become classics.

Fortunately for us, glimpses of many others—less classic—are preserved for future generations on these cards.

Tallahassee Auto Court in Capital City of Florida

65708

65 different and individual cottages with private baths

CABINS, COURTS, AND COTTAGES

Mohawk Park, Charlemont, Mass.

C abins and courts are the precursor to today's motels. In some ways the most modest form of temporary lodging, they could also be rather magical…your own miniature home away from home. Who wouldn't love to spend a night in a dollhouse such as that at Mohawk Park, Charlemont, Massachusetts, with its round-topped door, multipaned windows, and oversized chimney? Equally charming are the little "brick and marble" cottages with red-tiled roofs of the Tallahassee Auto Court.

It was important that these roadside hostelries be easily seen from cruising automobiles, so roofs were

Riverside Auto Court, Palmetto, Florida

← U. S. 41 →
← U. S. 541 →

Located on U. S. 41 and 541 — N. end of Manatee River Bridge, concrete construction, maple furniture, Venetian blinds, tile baths and steam heat, beautyrest mattresses and a radio in every room. Big attic fans make nights cool in summer. Mr. and Mrs. J. N. McClure, Owners and Operators.

UTAH MOTOR PARK
1000 South State Street
SALT LAKE CITY, UTAH

● Located in the Heart of the City. It covers five acres, beautifully parked with lawns, flowers and trees. **125 Modern Cottages** and a spacious **Club House** for all Guests.

often brightly colored. I had to include Bob's Bar-B-Q, Inc., because of his hypnotic checkered tiles. And I couldn't resist the endless perspective of little green-roofed cottages that formed just "Part of the English Village West, Indian Head, Franconia Notch, N.H."

Some groups of cabins had special attractions. Can you just imagine what the electrical and musical fountain at Nelson Dream Village must have sounded like?

Certain cards are endearing because they are so ridiculous. One wonders who chose the view of a driveway lined with white stones leading to a set of ordinary garages to advertise the Nevada Tourist Court. On the other hand, there is no questioning the charm of the Riverside Auto Court in Palmetto, Florida,

UTAH MOTOR PARK — SALT LAKE CITY, UTAH   4A-H475

BOB'S BAR-B-Q, INC.
ROLLING PRAIRIE, IND.

Indiana's Finest Modern Equipped CABINS and RESTAURANT. 24 Hour Service.

71 miles east of Chicago -- 175 miles west of Toledo
200 miles west of Detroit

Junction Routes 2 and 20

BOB'S BAR-B-Q, INC. — 18 MILES WEST OF SOUTH BEND, IND.

JUNCTION ROUTES 2 AND 20 — ONE OF THE CABIN DRIVES

7A-H1975

346L PART OF ENGLISH VILLAGE WEST, INDIAN HEAD, FRANCONIA NOTCH, N. H.
These attractive overnight bungalows are deluxe small homes with open fireplaces, over-stuffed furniture, excellent beds, modern baths with shower and screened sun porches. Shadow Lake offers swimming, boating and fishing.

13

which is all but smothered in flowers.

For all their modest size, many cabins advertised a multitude of features: maple furniture; Venetian blinds; tile baths; steam heat; Beautyrest mattresses; a radio in every room; big attic fans to make nights cool during the summer; carpeted floors; double cross-ventilation; telephone and Western Union service; a dining room serving food you'll remember; soft water; police protection; breeze-conditioned, scientifically built cabins modernistically created for beauty and comfort; private sunbathing; recommended by Duncan Hines. As one satisfied client of the Chapman Park Hotel and Bungalows wrote home, "Nothing second class to date... Really first class and mighty nice."

LEONARD & CATHERINE WHITE
Welcome You to

NEVADA TOURIST COURT

Drive in 200 Feet from U. S. 54
To Enjoy Our 20 MODERN UNITS
1 to 3 Rooms — 8 Garages — Shaded Lawns
— Playground — 1½ Blocks East of Business
District.
NEVADA, MISSOURI

200 Ft. from Highway — on U. S. 54 — 3 Blocks West of U. S. 71

Air-Cooled — NEVADA TOURIST COURT — Steam Heated

2C-H739

Famous for Pecans and Honey   Fishing - Hunting

Uvalde Courts - Uvalde, Texas

UVALDE COURTS
Uvalde, Texas
Located in the Center of the City
One Block West of the Plaza
On U. S. Highway 90
Strictly Modern Accommodations

ELECTRICAL AND MUSICAL FOUNTAIN

NELSON DREAM VILLAGE — U.S. HIGHWAY No. 66 AND No. 5 — LEBANON, MO.   6A-H769

NELSON DREAM VILLAGE
Annex To The FAMOUS NELSON TAVERN

See and hear the Musical Fountain
Cool Nights in the Ozark Mountains
Free Garage   Coffee Shop   Dining Room
Chicken Dinners A Specialty
Strictly Modern   Moderate Prices
The Gateway to the South and West
U. S. Highway No. 66 and No. 5
LEBANON, MO.

Good FISHING AND HUNTING *in Season*

DANN-DEE CAMP — PRESCOTT, ARIZONA   7A-H2388

DANN-DEE CAMP
PRESCOTT, ARIZONA

———

Eight blocks east of Court House
on Highway 89.
Modern conveniences at reasonable rates.

———

Clean Cottages Our Specialty.

Homestead Inn Annex, New Milford, Conn.

76006

y definition, an inn is a public lodging house serving food and drink to travelers. Many of the inns on linen cards have the appearance of having been private houses at one time, or have homelike atmospheres. Two attractive examples are the Homestead Inn Annex in New Milford, Connecticut, and the Valley Green Inn in Philadelphia. I have included a few examples of inns seeming to cater more specifically to

inns

170 VALLEY GREEN INN. WISSAHICKON DRIVE, PHILADELPHIA, PA.

VALLEY GREEN.

3A-H941

automobile travelers: the Midway Inn in Bedford, Pennsylvania, and the Mountain View Inn in Lahood Park, Montana. Two lovely cards show the attractive Santa Maria Inn in 1936 and 1940. How strikingly different the change in color scheme makes the same building look.

I especially like the card showing the early "stretch" station wagons outside the arched entrance of Montana's

Gallatin Gateway Inn, built in 1927 to house rail travelers on their way to nearby Yellowstone Park. Happily, the elegant Gallatin, which closed in the 1940s, has recently been lovingly restored.

The scene on the card showing the Paradise Inn at Mount Rainier National Park, Washington, could hardly be more dramatic with its entrance a tunnel through the snow and a dog team above.

The Turnpike's picturesque Midway Service Station at Bedford, with a tourist dining hall for 120 persons, dormitories and lunch room for drivers, and resident facilities for employees.

PA 115—The Turnpike's Picturesque Midway Inn and Service Station at Bedford
"America's Dream Highway"

MOUNTAIN VIEW INN,
LAHOOD PARK, MONTANA

This modern hotel "Headquarters for Morrison Cave" is located in beautiful Jefferson Canyon, near Morrison Cave State Park, on Highway U. S. 10S between Butte and Bozeman, Mont.

Mountain View Inn, Lahood Park, Montana

MODERN HOTEL—STEAM HEATED

Headquarters for Morrison Cave State Park, Montana

4B-H1363

DE

Between Norfolk and Cape Charles Ferry
Four Miles from Norfolk
Six Miles from Little Creek Ferry Terminal
Locked Garages Free — Famous for Food
Our Beds insure refreshing sleep
THE FOX HALL TOURIST INN

THE FOX HALL TOURIST INN
Mrs. Anna G. Sawyer, Hostess
ON ROUTE 460
NORFOLK, VA. 64217

INN, ELIZABETHTOWN, N. Y. 12AD

6A-H2729

The Inn, Silver Bay Association, Silver Bay, on Lake George, N. Y. 284

7A-H2396

19

SANTA MARIA INN
SANTA MARIA, CALIFORNIA
ON THE MISSION TRAIL
"IT IS ALWAYS BLOSSOM TIME
AT THE SANTA MARIA INN"

20

SANTA MARIA, CALIFORNIA

SANTA MARIA INN

Santa Maria's hotel facilities cover the range from the modest to most up-to-date metropolitan service. Here is pictured the SANTA MARIA INN, a hostelry famed throughout the world for its comfortable appointments and its cuisine.

M-10—Santa Maria Inn, Santa Maria, California

OB-H1495

21

RAINIER NATIONAL PARK

EARLY JULY AT PARADISE INN

28-547

7A-H789

Early July scene at Paradise Inn. Road has been opened by steamshovel. Inn is entered through tunnel. Alaska dog team on upper level. Stage is of the type operated from gateways to Park. Rainier National Park, Washington.

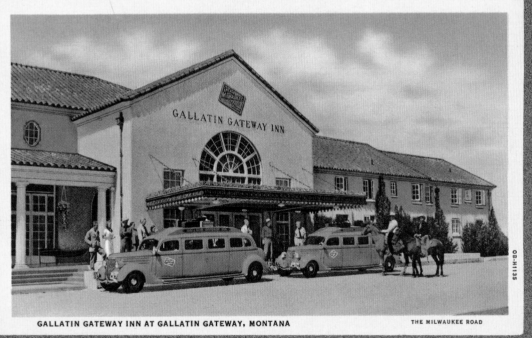

GALLATIN GATEWAY INN AT GALLATIN GATEWAY, MONTANA

THE MILWAUKEE ROAD

OB-H1135

CHICAGO
MILWAUKEE
ST. PAUL
AND PACIFIC

Thirty-five miles south of Three Forks, in the heart of the Montana Rockies at the head of Gallatin Canyon is The Milwaukee Road's hospitable Gallatin Gateway Inn... headquarters for western recreational activities and the northern entrance to Yellowstone Park.

WINTER SCENE IN YELLOWSTONE PARK SHOWING OLD FAITHFUL GEYSER AND OLD FAITHFUL INN

In both the United States and Canada we have strong romantic attachments to our pioneer past, in which mankind's cunning and fortitude conquered nature's brute strength. The fantasy persists that beyond the city's borders and at the edge of the freeway the Great Outdoors remains ready to restore the soul weary of the city's never-ending roar. Indeed we are blessed with vast tracts of more or less virgin land pre-

LODGES

served through the wisdom of governments of an earlier era. The first of the United States' great national parks, Yellowstone, was dedicated in 1872. Others followed, and to make them accessible, a whole series of spectacular hotels was developed, built with natural materials and beautifully designed to give the visitor a sense of the grandeur of the site, while providing every modern comfort. The Old Faithful Inn, built in 1902–1903, with its impressive sloping roof, is a perfect foil for the famous geyser in the beautiful card Teich printed in 1937. The Ahwahnee, pictured in 1935, sits stolid among lush woods, dwarfed by the sheer vertical rocks that loom above it.

Canada's motto, *Ad Mare Usque Ad Mari*, From Sea to Sea, became a reality in 1886, when the first railroad line was completed by the Canadian Pacific Railroad Company. It linked Montreal, in the eastern province of Quebec, to Vancouver, in the Pacific west, some 3,000 miles away. From a few dining stations in the rugged Rockies, a group of magnificent resort hotels sprang up. Some, such as the impressive Glacier Park Hotel in British Columbia, were built of enormous logs with interior spaces of cyclopean proportions. But even here it was Man over Nature as well as Man over Native: the hotel's front yard enclosed a group of tepees. "Indian Days" was one of the attractions at the majestic Banff Springs Hotel, one of the stately hotels built in the French château style that became ubiquitous throughout the Dominion.

PHOTO BY HILEMAN

1071 GLACIER PARK HOTEL, GLACIER NATIONAL PARK   5A-H183

PHOTO BY HILEMAN

8017 LAKE McDONALD HOTEL, GLACIER NATIONAL PARK   5A-H200

1098—Lobby, Glacier Park Hotel, Glacier National Park

1B-H2497

25

The Canadian Rockies were dubbed the Canadian Alps, and the Prince of Wales Hotel in Waterton Lakes National Park, Alberta, was the chalet to end all chalets with its steeply pitched roof, balcony on top of balcony on top of yet more balconies, decorative timberwork, and giant brackets, all topped by a lookout spire. From the outside, it lends enchantment to the view of the surrounding mountains, and the stunning vista from the lofty lobby is captured in one of my favorite cards, in the chapter on The Grand Foyer.

26

PHOTO BY HILEMAN

6512   PRINCE OF WALES HOTEL, WATERTON LAKES NATIONAL PARK, ALBERTA, CANADA

7A-H494

The Ahwahnee is Yosemite's new hotel. It
is located on the north side of the valley
near the Royal Arches and from its location
commands all the major views of the valley.

YOSEMITE NATIONAL PARK

348

THE AHWAHNEE

5A-H176

27

28

OB-H932

Swimming Pool, El Mirador, Palm Springs, California

While some hotels provided food and lodging for travelers in transit, businesspeople, or visitors from out of town, others were designed as vacation spots, destinations in themselves. Often these were located by the water, in the mountains, or in other scenic areas. The resorts often provided such amenities as golf courses, swimming pools, horseback riding, therapeutic hot springs, tennis courts, nature trails, gourmet din-

THE GREAT RESORTS

29

ing, entertainment, and casinos. In the latter half of the nineteenth century, the affluent fled oppressive city summers to vacation spots in cooler climes such as Saratoga Springs, New York, or Cape May, New Jersey. The opulent Grand Union Hotel in Saratoga Springs provided private suites as well as rooms for guests, elegant parlors, ballrooms, dining facilities, and gardens, along with a 450-foot-long colonnaded terrace where one could hobnob with social peers while looking out on the passing parade.

If the Grand Union's porch seems impressive, it was nothing compared to that of another Grand: the Grand Hotel on Mackinac Island, Michigan, where guests could promenade along a piazza 700 feet long under a roof supported by forty three-story columns.

Changes in building techniques, the development of

the steel structure and the passenger elevator allowed buildings to expand upward, not merely outward. In the early years of this century, enormous multistoried beachfront hotels such as the Marlborough-Blenheim, Traymore, and Ambassador rose in Atlantic City, providing holiday facilities for the middle classes. Now most of these are gone, victims of changing tastes and fortune. Looking at the images of them that remain, it is hard to fathom how today's travelers can be content with the bland architecture of so many of our more up-to-date hotels; we seem embarrassed

North Frontage, Greenbrier Hotel, White Sulphur Springs, W. Va.

6A-H1563

THE RIVIERA — SHOWING SWIMMING POOL, SAND BEACH, AND TROPICAL GARDENS

9A-H818

FLORIDA'S FOREMOST ALL YEAR HOTEL NEAR DAYTONA

GRAND HOTEL AND GROUNDS, MACKINAC ISLAND, MICH.

3A-H1359

by the kind of opulence our parents and grandparents considered de rigueur.

Atlantic City's resort hotels may have reflected the scale and style of urban buildings of the Northeast, but in the South the traditional elegance of the antebellum plantation house was the model for the lovely Greenbrier Hotel in White Sulphur Springs, West Virginia, built in 1910. Its fine proportions, graceful portico, and four-story columns give it a timeless quality, beautifully captured in its portrait on page 30.

THE AMBASSADOR HOTEL
LOS ANGELES

A Twenty-Two Acre Playground in the Heart of a Great City offers endless opportunity for healthful recreation — tennis, golf, and the wonderful Lido with its Sun-tan sand bathing beach and crystal clear plunge. Home of the World Famous "Cocoanut Grove" where smart set and cinema stars mingle nightly.

THE AMBASSADOR HOTEL, CRYSTAL PLUNGE and SUNTAN BEACH, LOS ANGELES, CALIFORNIA

7A-H2257

HOTEL BREAKERS
CORPUS CHRISTI, TEXAS
"The Naples of the Gulf"
All Outside Rooms
Private Tub and Shower Baths
Recreation Hall—Coffee Shop—Bathers Lounge
Surf Bathing from Your Room

32

HOTEL BREAKERS

THE ONLY HOTEL ON THE BEACH

CORPUS CHRISTI, TEXAS

HOTEL BREAKERS

PRIVATE FISHING AND PLEASURE PIER

DELIGHTFUL SUMMER AND WINTER

9-A-H465

OWN PRIVATE BEACH

TWO BLOCKS LONG

FREE FROM UNDERTOW

HOTEL PALOMAR, Santa Cruz, California
New — Modern — Fireproof
ANDY BALICH, Owner
Located in the Heart of a Paradise of Nature
Where Every Outdoor Recreation Awaits You.

HOTEL PALOMAR

SANTA CRUZ, CALIFORNIA

NEW · MODERN · FIREPROOF

SA-H696

33

The Broadmoor in Colorado Springs, Colorado, is one of those hotels that, once seen, is never forgotten. The offset tower, gently sloping roofline, and canted corners of the main block soften the formality of the architectural composition. The rugged Rocky Mountains form a perfect foil for the dazzling white walls, and the enchantment is further enhanced by the blue Colorado sky and fluffy Teich clouds.

Two cards are included in this section not for the excellence of the architecture but because of the sheer funkiness of their execution. The Hotel Breakers in Corpus Christi, Texas, has little to distinguish it architecturally, but whoever drew those figures on the pier and the sailboat that appears to be about to sail into the sky certainly had a good time. (People appearing in salesmen's original photographs were always airbrushed out or

GRAND UNION HOTEL. SARATOGA SPRINGS. N. Y.   4

5   HOTEL TRAYMORE AND BOARDWALK, ATLANTIC CITY, N. J.

3A-H1217

altered so that they could not be recognized, unless a photographic release had been signed.) The vaguely *japonaise* beach scenes that frame the Hotel Palomar in Santa Cruz, California, make this another of my favorite Teich cards.

The Los Angeles Ambassador Hotel, whose swimming pool fronted its Lido Club with curiously Egyptian columns, was home of the Cocoanut Grove, one of the most famous nightclubs of the 1930s and 1940s. Charlie Chaplin swam here, Errol Flynn lived in a bungalow within the hotel's twenty-two acres of manicured lawns and gardens, and Joan Crawford entered dance contests in its heyday. The Ambassador opened in 1921 and is currently threatened with demolition. The smart set has moved on.

31 MARLBOROUGH-BLENHEIM HOTEL, ATLANTIC CITY, N. J.

3AH-1229

35

Hotel Kenmore · Commonwealth Ave · At Kenmore Square · Boston 15 · Massachusetts

One way in which hotels of the first three or four decades of this century differed from those that followed was in their continued homage to the historical styles that have been the basis of Western architecture since the golden age of Greece, 2,500 years ago.

Many of these buildings are visually comforting because they conformed to the traditional, and logical,

CITY HOTELS

order of base, shaft, and top. The decorative vocabulary of the ancients included naturalistic elements based on rosettes, laurel branches and wreaths, garlands of fruit and flowers, shells, acanthus leaves, and dolphins, as well as man-made objects such as masks, urns, ribbons, disks, torches, helmets, ropes, and obelisks. In the last decade there has been an encouraging revival of some of the basic elements of classical architecture, often used in an unconventional, almost tongue-in-cheek manner. Alas, the joke often falls a little flat, especially when we compare the results to the sources from which they derive. What we admire in so many of the buildings of the twenties and thirties are the very sculptural elements that were swept away as extraneous when the modern movement accepted the dictum Form Follows Function. But is beauty not a function, too?

It is amazing to see how well historical design stood up to the stretching it received when skyscrapers made

HOTEL
ST. FRANCIS

HOTEL
ST FRANCIS

REEN CO. DRUGS

SAINT FRANCIS HOTEL — ST. PAUL, MINNESOTA

5A-H837

38

SAINT FRANCIS HOTEL
ST. PAUL, MINNESOTA
—
COMPLETELY REFURNISHED, REDECORATED
MODERN AND FIREPROOF

their debut. Tall shafts were enlivened with ornamental balconies, escutcheons or shields, decorative brickwork, and a variety of window frames and pediments. Thus city skylines were enhanced with romantic mansard roofs and corner towers, such as those on New York's Plaza Hotel, or fanciful spires capped with classical lanterns such as those on the Sherry Netherlands,

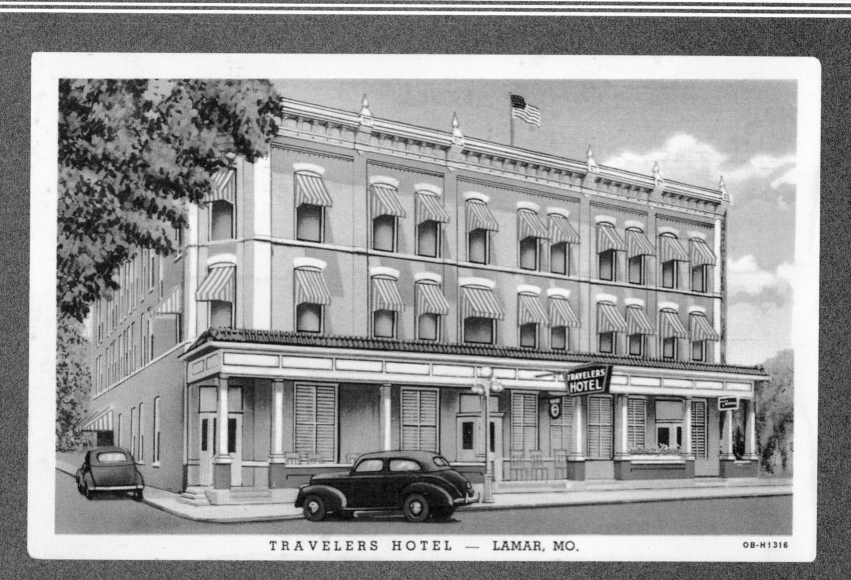

TRAVELERS HOTEL — LAMAR, MO.

OB-H1316

New York, the Miami Biltmore in Coral Gables, Florida, or the Claridge in Atlantic City. Other rooflines were decorated with rows of Greek palmettes, heavy projecting cornices, balustrades, or columned pavilions.

The architects of these high-rise hotels had thousands of years of architectural styles to draw on. Variations on French or Italian Renaissance palaces were very popu-

Travelers Hotel · **LAMAR MISSOURI**

★ Is known to thousands as one of the most beautiful hotels in western Missouri. Located on U. S. Highways 160 and 71 at the gateway to the Ozarks makes it an ideal stopping place. Large and cheerful rooms. Excellent dining room service.

— *Popular Prices* —

40

6B-H2053

This fine building is the largest and most modern hotel in the Black Hills Region, serving the many thousands visitors of the world famous Big Bad Lands and Black Hills of South Dakota.

The hotel is centrally located in the city and many tourists can make their headquarters here for interesting trips to the Bad Lands and in the Black Hills.

Hotel Algonquin
Port Huron, Michigan

ZC-H1179

lar, especially in the East, while the Spanish influence seemed appropriate for Florida and California. Occasionally we find variations on Moorish (Hotel Algonquin, Port Huron, Michigan) or north European half-timbered as in the Alex Johnson Hotel in Rapid City, South Dakota, which to me looks like an English stately home with a thyroid problem.

MT. EVANS (ALT. 14,260 FT.) AND RANGE FROM BEAR CREEK VALLEY

THE OXFORD HOTEL

DENVER, COLORADO

MT. EVANS, TWO HOURS DRIVE FROM THE OXFORD HOTEL, DENVER, COLO.

6A-H2825

42

DESIGN COPYRIGHTS RESERVED BY HOTEL CONVERSE

5A-H305

43

HOTEL CONVERSE
325 First Street -- Niagara Falls, N. Y.

● This new modern hotel of one hundred rooms, sixty-five with private bath, offers accommodations of the better type at rates within reach of all. Its location, just two blocks from the great Falls of Niagara is so central that it makes the ideal stopping place.

Under Ownership Management -- H. S. Converse, Mgr.

AN ENTIRE CITY BLOCK OF HOSPITALITY

PANTLIND HOTEL — GRAND RAPIDS, MICHIGAN

5A-H1480

The PANTLIND HOTEL
has 750 rooms, Continental dining room, cafeteria and men's grill. A floor of seven foot beds for tall people.

Excellent Convention Facilities

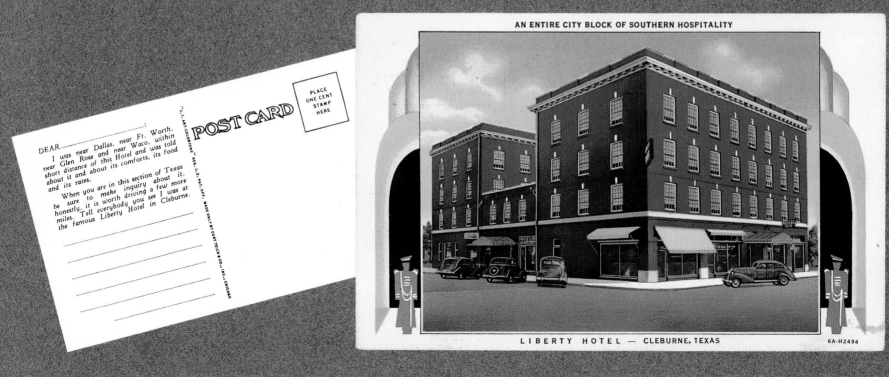

DEAR_____:
I was near Dallas, near Ft. Worth, near Glen Rose and near Waco, within short distance of this Hotel and was told about it and about its comforts, its food and its rates.

When you are in this section of Texas be sure to make inquiry about it, honestly, it is worth driving a few more miles. Tell everybody you see I was at the famous Liberty Hotel in Cleburne.

POST CARD

PLACE ONE CENT STAMP HERE

"C.T. ART-COLORTONE" REG. U.S. PAT. OFF. MADE ONLY BY CURT TEICH & CO., INC., CHICAGO

AN ENTIRE CITY BLOCK OF SOUTHERN HOSPITALITY

LIBERTY HOTEL — CLEBURNE, TEXAS

6A-H2494

HOTEL MUEHLEBACH — KANSAS CITY, MISSOURI

2A-H306

45

HOTEL INDIANA   FORT WAYNE, INDIANA

THE MAROTT APARTMENT HOTEL, NORTH

JEFFERSON HOTEL
Franklin, Jefferson and Main Streets
RICHMOND, VA.

This magnificent Hotel was first opened to public patronage in 1895 it was erected by the late Maj. Lewis Ginter, at a cost of nearly two million dollars. It is not surpassed in point of architectural beauty and completeness of equipment by any other hotel in the Country. Ideally situated in the most desirable section of Richmond, within five minutes walk of the business center and shopping district.

JEFFERSON HOTEL. RICHMOND. VA.

60397

AT FALL CREEK BOULEVARD, INDIANAPOLIS, IND.

Hotel Florence — Missoula, Montana   "America's Finest Small Hotel"

3A-H752

24— Hotel Peabody, Memphis, Tenn.

6A-H2014

Hotel Florence
"America's Finest Small Hotel"
MISSOULA, MONTANA
150 Modern Rooms. Temperature Controlled
Air-Conditioning Throughout.

MISSOULA, MONT.
MAR 19
12 M
1952

32:-LORD BALTIMORE HOTEL. HANOVER AND BALTIMORE STS..

BALTIMORE. MD.   44454

THE COLUMBUS   MIAMI, FLORIDA

OVERLOOKING BAYFRONT PARK

8A-H3158

Hotel WESTWARD HO

"In the Valley of the Sun"

AIR COOLED   P H O E N I X   350 ROOMS

7A-H2841

THE HARRISBURGER -- HARRISBURG, PA.

The DESHLER WALLICK HOTEL is one of Columbus' most modern hotels. It contains 1,000 rooms and baths; 600 of these rooms are located in the 45 story Le Veque-Lincoln Tower.

A8—Deshler Wallick Hotel, R.K.O. Theatre and Le Veque-Lincoln Tower

Columbus, Ohio

135

CONGRESS HOTEL, CHICAGO

4A-H351

HOTEL CLEVELAND
In the Heart of Cleveland

Directly connected with Union Passenger Terminal and Terminal Tower.

Observation porch on 42nd floor of Tower affords a panoramic view of Cleveland— Lake Erie to the north, industrial Cleveland to the south, and residential Cleveland to the east and west.

NEW HOTEL JEFFERSON · THE ARISTOCRAT OF ST. LOUIS

ST. LOUIS, MO.

3A-H332

HOTEL CLEVELAND
CLEVELAND, OHIO

Certain hotels are from their inception destined to achieve the title of supreme respect: Grand Hotel. Architecturally distinguished by fine design, excellence of detail, and sumptuousness of materials; impeccably maintained, equipped with the finest of dining rooms, salons, ballrooms, and lounges; easily accessible to the most select shops and cultural attractions in town—these highly esteemed commercial enterprises fill an important position as social center and meeting place within their communities. One has only to mention certain names...the Waldorf Astoria and the Plaza in New York, the Palmer House in Chicago, the

77 PARK PLAZA AND HOTEL CHASE, ST. LOUIS, MO.

2A-H1048

The new Park Plaza Hotel, of especially distinctive architecture, and the Chase Hotel, two of the apartment hotels which overlook Forest Park, one of the world's finest parks.

GRAND HOTELS

The Sherry Netherlands, Savoy Hilton from Central Park Lake,

New York City

189   62297

Waldorf Astoria Hotel. Park Ave. & 50th St., New York City

K4004   324

SHERRY NETHERLANDS SAVOY HILTON
FROM CENTRAL PARK LAKE
Most every visitor to New York City takes a trip through
Central Park. It comprises 840 acres and is surrounded on all
sides by beautiful Hotels and Apartment Houses. Here in a
beautiful view across Central Park Lake are shown the well known
Sherry Netherlands and the Savoy Hilton.

The Waldorf-Astoria
is the largest and the tallest hotel in the world.
The building covers 81,337 square feet . . . is 47
stories high with twin towers bringing the total
height to 625 feet 7 inches.

M-108 MIAMI BILTMORE HOTEL, CORAL GABLES, FLA.

PHOTO BY MANLEY BROWER

5A-H907

FAIRMONT HOTEL

Nob Hill, San Francisco

7A-H1408

Miami Biltmore in Coral Gables, the Jefferson in Richmond, Virginia, the Breakers in Palm Beach, the Fairmont and Mark Hopkins in San Francisco, the Royal York in Toronto, the Château Frontenac in Quebec, the Ritz-Carlton in Montreal, these and a score of others conjure up images of grace, splendor, and pride. Nor is it just in the larger cities that hotels fill such a social position. One should not visit Boulder without enjoying the grand wooden staircase and glass ceiling in the Boulderado, or Santa Fe without enjoying the neo-adobe public rooms and courtyard of La Fonda.

Not all Grand Hotels are represented on Teich cards. Some chose more select paper and styles of representation to separate themselves from the average or merely good hotel. And not all hotels photograph well. Few city streets are wide enough to allow a camera the distance to capture block-long façades in their entirety. But some linen cards exist that graphically portray their subjects with all the dignity they deserve. At one time the Sherry

The Copley Plaza ~ Boston

85 Hotel Claridge, Atlantic City, N. J.

Netherlands, Savoy Plaza, and Plaza formed an elegant trio clustered around the southeastern corner of Central Park. The first two are captured in charming juxtaposition on one card. Sadly, this view is gone forever due to the destruction in the 1960s of the Savoy Plaza and its replacement by a graceless office box.

The Park Plaza in St. Louis, Missouri, has great presence in the card on which both it and the Hotel Chase are featured. Its architectural composition features the kind of symmetrical setback blocks typical of the 1920s, with decorative elements capping each step and the whole giving the effect of a great pyramid crowned with a temple. The retouch artist has used great skill in treating the shadows to help reveal the shape of the building.

Boston's Copley Plaza's rather squat proportions are relieved by a large central bow flanked by symmetrical columned entry porches and graceful tall arched windows on the ground floor. The skywritten message is a novel touch.

Jokake Inn— is a Winter Resort Hotel situated on the Desert, on the "sunny side" of Camel Back Mountain. The Inn is appropriately executed in Mexican and Indian architecture, and is ten miles from the center of Phoenix, Capital and largest city in Arizona.

P-31

Jokake Inn, near Phoenix, Arizona

9A-H274

SOUTHWEST STYLE

p-60

Camelback Inn, near Phoenix, Arizona, is said to be one of the world's most picturesque winter resorts—an Oasis on the Desert "where time stands still."

Entrance to Camelback Inn, Phoenix, Arizona

57

6B-H29

The 1980s saw what is known as "Santa Fe Style" become a major decorating trend. Typical elements include adobe-colored, softly contoured walls; exposed-log ceiling beams or *vegas*; projecting drain spouts or *canales*; floors of brick, stone, tile, or pine; rustic handcrafted colonial furniture; and a palette of earth tones highlighted with delightful turquoise, cobalt blue, red, and whitewash. But what we are seeing

P-33   Arizona Biltmore, Phoenix, Arizona

6A-H705

58

The Hotels in the "Valley of the Sun" are among the country's finest. The Arizona Biltmore is one of the most prominent, a luxurious Hotel surrounded with well appointed bungalows in spacious gardens, offering every convenience to its guests who have come to Arizona to rest and play, and above all to be in the sun.

P-30   Patio of The Arizona Biltmore, Phoenix, Arizona

9A-H273

59

The Arizona Biltmore, world renowned for
its superb service and its excellent standards
of hospitality, a triumph in modern architecture, is located in the heart of the Arizona
desert, near Phoenix, Arizona.

"The Meadows" as it is familiarly known, is a hostelry in the best southwestern style, typifying the spirit of Las Vegas, which is the gateway to some of the most beautiful mountains, canyons, waterfalls and scenic grandeur in the entire country.
— PHOTO BY PAUL ODOR

LA FONDA HOTEL, SANTA FE, NEW MEXICO

This new modern hostelry—operated by Fred Harvey—built on the lines of and maintaining both Indian and Old Spanish architecture, is the most unique and picturesque in the entire Southwest. Furnished with Spanish and Indian antiques and authentic reproductions, it is a veritable storehouse of information for the student.

The sketch below is of the original La Fonda which stood on the same site at the end of the Santa Fe Trail.

now is a revival of a revival that became popular in the 1920s, when there was a reversal of the trend in the West toward the importation of building materials and styles from the industrial East, and a return to the architecture that combined Native American and colonial Spanish influences.

Designers of hotels in New Mexico and Arizona responded to this regional look; not only did the thick walls, small windows, and native materials make sense—as they had for hundreds of years in this area of climatic extremes—but the romance of the Old West was an attraction for vacationers from the East seeking a change

LA CAVERNA HOTEL
Carlsbad, New Mexico
Gateway to Carlsbad Caverns

Carlsbad Cavern National Park is open every day in the year. Accessible to Southern Transcontinental routes.

La Caverna—nearest hotel to the Cavern—is modern and architecturally interesting.

Rates surprisingly low

Hunting   Golf   Fishing

FRANCISCAN,
ALBUQUERQUE, NEW MEXICO

This structure, typical of the architecture brought to the Southwest by the early settlers, is regarded as the most unusual building of its type anywhere in the world. It was built by the Community Spirit of Albuquerque. The Hotel contains 175 guest rooms. Its lobby, magnificently decorated, is the most artistic interior in this section of the country. The Hotel is especially adapted to the entertainment of Clubs, Conventions and large social gatherings. Every attention is paid to the comfort of cross country tourists, whose prolonged stay is desirable to all Albuquerque.

CARLSBAD N.M. MAY 1 1935

LA CAVERNA HOTEL — CARLSBAD, NEW MEXICO   3A-H456

FRANCISCAN HOTEL

from their everyday city lives. What more natural destination could there be for a traveler on the Santa Fe Railroad than the cool and beautiful adobe-style La Fonda Hotel, with its antique Spanish and Indian furnishings.

An interesting variation on the Southwest style is seen in the modernistic Arizona Biltmore in Phoenix, whose architecture is a dramatic synthesis of Toltec and Wrightian influences, the latter especially evident in the view from the courtyard. The more traditional Meadows Hotel in Las Vegas leans toward the pure Spanish mission style, with richly decorated surfaces played against warm expanses of creamy stucco.

R-57   ROTUNDA WING, MISSION INN, RIVERSIDE, CALIFORNIA

2A-H135

EL CORDOVA HOTEL   CORONADO, CALIFORNIA

CAVALIER HOTEL

SUPERBLY LOCATED ON THE OCEAN FRONT

7A-H1425

63

There are two main architectural directions in Florida's hotels. First, and earlier, is the historical approach developed most notably by the extraordinarily talented Addison Mizner, whose charming re-creations of Mediterranean villages were so effective in glamorizing Palm Beach. Mizner was not only an imaginative designer and decorator, but also a canny businessman who created workshops where he manu-

FLORIDA, LAND OF SUNSHINE

THE CLEVELANDER   MIAMI BEACH, FLORIDA

SOLARIUM

CLEVELANDER

Private Beach Service   Directly On The Ocean

64

9A-H2041

THE CLEVELANDER
On the Ocean between 10th and 11th Streets
MIAMI BEACH, FLORIDA

factured suitable "antiques" to furnish the opulent villas he created for the very rich and famous.

The second architectural wave was a populist form of Art Deco, the style first introduced at, and named after the Exposition des Arts Décoratifs in Paris in 1925. Elements of Parisian chic were married to a range of delightful maritime motifs to create a world of confectionary modernity for middle-class sun seekers in Miami Beach. Of all the linen cards in my collection, I find these Miami fantasies the most engaging.

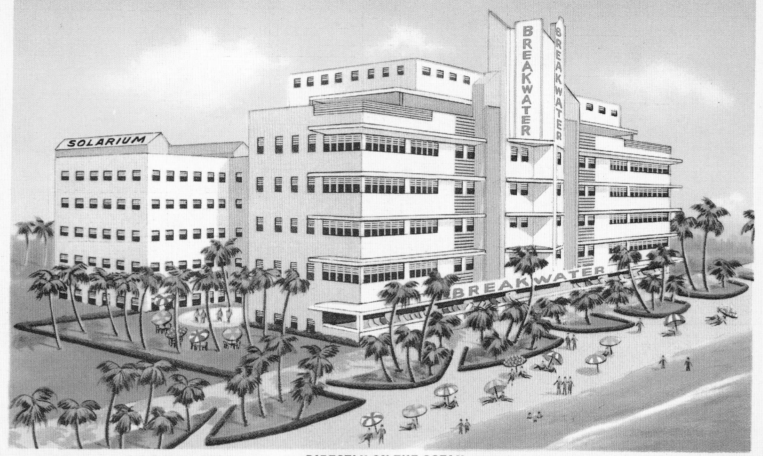

BREAKWATER HOTEL   MIAMI BEACH, FLORIDA

SOLARIUM

BREAKWATER

BREAKWATER

DIRECTLY ON THE OCEAN   9A-H2428

BREAKWATER HOTEL
On the Ocean at 10th Street
MIAMI BEACH, FLORIDA
Vacation Paradise — The right people awarded over-
whelming recognition to this New Hotel as the Smart-
est on the Beach — European Plan —

Not only are the hotels themselves totally charming, but I marvel at the wealth of detail packed into each card. Palm trees, patios, ocean surf, sandy beaches, sun umbrellas, bathing beauties, speedboats, strolling lovers, streamlined roadsters, swimming pools, and riotous gardens happily combine to create a world that is truly a tropical paradise. And fortunately, many of these delightful minor masterpieces of hotel design have been recently restored for the pleasure of another generation of "snow birds" escaping from northern winters.

THE MARINE TERRACE HOTEL   MIAMI BEACH, FLORIDA

ON THE OCEAN   6A-H497

It takes a second glance to realize that the three cards grouped here all represent the same hotel, the Marine Terrace, at different stages of development. The two-tone sand-colored façade with the inverted arches along the roofline appears on a card from 1936. A year later the roofline appears simplified and the building has been painted all white. By 1939, a wing has been added, and patrons are shown enjoying rooftop dining and dancing under the palms. The blurb on the back of the earliest card subtly mentions that the hotel is in an "Exclusive Section." Later, the phrase "Selected clientele" is added. The final card blatantly advertises "Strictly Gentile." The management of 1939 would plotz if they could see the mix of today's Miami Beach vacationers.

THE MARINE TERRACE HOTEL   MIAMI BEACH, FLORIDA

ON THE OCEAN AND WITH PRIVATE BEACH   7AH1074

THE MARINE TERRACE HOTEL

MIAMI BEACH, FLORIDA

DIRECTLY ON THE OCEAN — PRIVATE BEACH

9A-H2305

THE MARINE TERRACE HOTEL
On the Oceanfront at 27th Street
MIAMI BEACH, FLORIDA
Strictly Gentile Clientele — All Outside Rooms with
Bath — Dining and Dancing Patio — Parking Facilities —
Open the year around —
PRIVATE BEACH

67

CONGRESS HOTEL

MIAMI BEACH, FLORIDA

ON THE OCEAN

6A-H2208

Although I hate to destroy a beautiful illusion, the truth is that not everything we see in these delightful Miami cards was exactly the same as it was in real life. Very often a hotel located four or five or six blocks from the beach wanted to pretend that it was right on the water. So it was very common to take a picture and strip in the beach right at the front door. But then, a little walk in the sunshine never hurt anyone.

PETER MILLER HOTEL
Collins Ave. at 19th
MIAMI BEACH, FLA.
The Ultimate in a Modern Hotel — Overlooking the
Ocean and a Short Walk to the Theatre and Shopping
Center—

69

PETER MILLER HOTEL

MIAMI BEACH, FLORIDA

6A-H2881

HOTEL ASTOR

MIAMI BEACH, FLORIDA

HOTEL ASTOR

OVERLOOKING OCEAN

6A-H1971

70

HOTEL ASTOR
Cor. 10th St. and Washington Ave.
MIAMI BEACH
An Ultra-Modern hotel — All rooms with private
bath and shower, telephone — Every room exquisitely
furnished — Spacious Lobby — Sun Parlor — Elevator
— Steam Heat — Sun Porch — Solarium —

THE SHOREHAM.

MIAMI BEACH, FLORIDA

ON THE OCEAN

71

S-141—Vinoy Park Hotel, St. Petersburg, Fla.

5A-H1062

S-153   THE DON CE-SAR BEACH HOTEL, ON THE GUL

NEAR ST. PETERSBURG, FLA.

H-104   TROPICAL TREES AND FLOWERS ON LAWN OF HOLLYWOOD BEACH HOTEL

HOLLYWOOD, FLA.

4A-H649

ICO, PASS-A-GRILLE

4A-H805

BEAUTIFUL GARDENS AND FLOWERS   ENTRANCE TO BREAKERS HOTEL

PALM BEACH, FLORIDA

11962

M-223   THE RONEY PLAZA HOTEL, MIAMI BEACH, FLA.

PHOTO BY BERRY-HILTON CO.

3A-H573

Hotel Ponce De Leon, St. Augustine, Florida   10 N

The Oldest City in the United States

HOTEL PONCE DE LEON, ST. AUGUSTINE, FLORIDA
The Oldest City in the United States
The first great resort hotel of Florida's East Coast Hotel
System, was started by Henry M. Flagler in 1885. Completed in 1888, costing about two and a half million. Its
Spanish Moorish buildings and magnificent grounds surrounding them cover about 13 acres of reclaimed land in
the heart of the city. Royalty, Presidents and other famous
personages have been its guests.

D. C. 145—Ocean Front Hotel Barracks, Army Air Forces, Miami Beach, Fla.

VERSAILLES HOTEL
WHITMAN HOTEL
SEA ISLE HOTEL
SHOREMEDE HOTEL
OCEAN GRANDE HOTEL
CARIBBEAN HOTEL
PANCOAST HOTEL

2B-H1364

THIS SPACE FOR WRITING MESSAGES

BUY
WAR SAVINGS
POSTCARD
STAMPS

Pvt. George Zulu
4022 Eng. H.
Flight 0-37 B. F784
Miami Beach, Florida

"Hello Pop. Are
you feeling well. You
ought to be in Miami
Beach with me. I live
in a hotel room. I
get off every night. I'm
having a swell time
Love, George

Mr. James Z
1364 Gat
Brooklyn

Lobby — HOTEL ELLIOTT — DES MOINES, IOWA

7A-H2363

iews of the hotel lobbies are rare and fascinating. Foyers are multipurpose spaces: greeting place; meeting place; lounge; waiting room; business, information, and message centers; entryway to various public and private areas; access to elevators and stairs; and finally, departure lounge. It is here that one's first and last impressions of the establishment are made. As a result, the foyer is often the most extravagant and imagi-

THE GRAND FOYER

ST. LOUIS, MO.   2A-H1014

76

natively designed space in the building, and whatever the style of the decor, it is here that it is most fully expressed.

Even a modest hotel such as the Elliott in Des Moines, Iowa, was able to respond to the dernier cri in interior design through clever striping on the walls and careful choice of colors for its paneled ceiling. The artistic treat-

ment of the clock over the reception desk, a round cobalt-blue mirror, and a pair of smart *torchère* lamps complete the ensemble and distract from the rather banal armchairs.

The enormous New Hotel Jefferson in St. Louis, Missouri, produced a number of cards of its various public rooms (see The Rendezvous, pages 86 and 87). Its Grand

"THE PALM COURT" — THE ROOSEVELT — NEW YORK

5A-H594

77

Lobby is a splendid space of massive columns, arched ceiling with arboreal motifs, bronze railings, decorative sconces, and potted plants. The Palm Court of the Roosevelt, in New York, is one of the loveliest public rooms, with its delicate blue-and-gold color scheme, fine paneling, tall Corinthian columns with gilded capitals, gold shaded chandelier, and palms in Oriental pots.

The Roosevelt

45TH AND MADISON AVE. -- NEW YORK CITY

THE PALM COURT, located at the south end of the lobby, is considered one of the most beautiful rooms in New York, special attention having been given the decorations to give it a restful atmosphere, while the profusion of palms and foliage also lend their attraction. Tea is served each afternoon in the Palm Court and an excellent string orchestra renders classical and popular music.

WEST LOUNGE — EDGEWATER BEACH HOTEL — 5300 BLOCK-SHERIDAN ROAD — CHICAGO 1A-H147

The word *foyer* derives from the Latin word for *hearth*, and the massive hearth is the centerpiece of the spectacular West Lounge of Chicago's Edgewater Beach Hotel.

Located on Lake Michigan, the hotel was built with 1,000 guest rooms, a 200-car garage, extensive lawns and gardens, children's play room, putting course, tennis

PHOTO BY HILEMAN

6514 LOBBY, PRINCE OF WALES HOTEL, WATERTON LAKES NATIONAL PARK, ALBERTA, CANADA

7A-H492

courts, private bathing beach, open-air marble dance floor, and a 1,000-foot-long beach promenade.

The vertical scale of the chalet-styled Prince of Wales Hotel in Waterton Lakes National Park, Alberta, Canada, is emphasized by a view in which both interior comfort and the grandeur of the setting are revealed.

LOBBY — HOTEL ATLANTIC — CLARK ST. NEAR JACKSON BOULEVARD — CHICAGO

HOTEL ATLANTIC
Famous for Good Cooking
450 Rooms — 300 with Bath
$2.00 a day and up
Clark Street near Jackson Boulevard
CHICAGO

HOTEL ATLANTIC
Famous for Good Cooking
450 Rooms — 300 with Bath
$2.00 a day and up
CLARK STREET NEAR JACKSON BOULEVARD
CHICAGO

LOBBY — HOTEL ATLANTIC — CLARK ST. NEAR JACKSON BOULEVARD — CHICAGO

THE ATLANTAN
Cone and Luckie Streets
DOWNTOWN ATLANTA
Air Conditioned Rooms, Lobby and Restaurant

The Atlantan Hotel
ATLANTA, GA.

LOBBY
HARRISON HOTEL
CHICAGO'S NEWEST

HARRISON HOTEL
Drive-In Garage Connects with Lobby

400 Rooms — 400 Baths
Free Radio — Circulating Ice Water
HARRISON ST. OFF MICHIGAN BLVD.

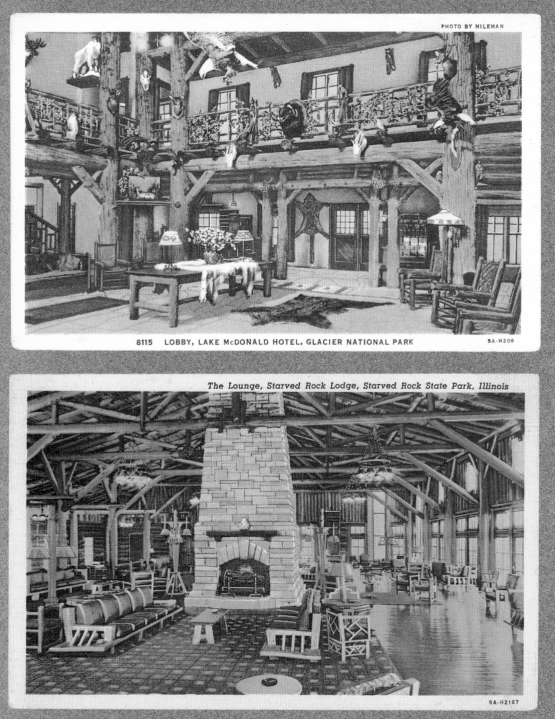

PHOTO BY HILEMAN

8115   LOBBY, LAKE McDONALD HOTEL, GLACIER NATIONAL PARK

5A-H208

The Lounge, Starved Rock Lodge, Starved Rock State Park, Illinois

9A-H2167

PHOTO BY HILEMAN

1B-H2498

4222—Lobby, Many Glacier Hotel, Glacier National Park

BROOK THROUGH WORLD FAMOUS DINING ROOM, BROOKDALE LODGE, BROOKDALE, CALIF.   921

© STANLEY A. PILTZ   3B-H622

One of the delights when traveling is to be able to enjoy an out-of-this-world dinner in a restaurant with drop-dead decor worth writing home about and to enjoy a glamorous evening of exotic drinks and dancing in some fabulous (and famous) sky-top lounge with live music just like the big bands on the radio.

Well, here they are, folks: gorgeous supper clubs with real fake palms and Oriental lanterns and saturn light

DINNER, DRINKS, AND DANCING

HOTEL RACINE — *MANDALAY LOUNGE and BAR* — RACINE, WISCONSIN   2B-H878

Coffee Shop — HOTEL BENTLEY — ALEXANDRIA, LA.

The Trocadero, most famous Reno supper club, is one of the highlights of your visit to Western Nevada. Excellent food and superb cocktails at the Trocadero, Hotel El Cortez, Reno.

globes and ceilings with stars that twinkle; little round tables with leatherette chairs—just like in the movies; merry-go-round bars where you can drink a pink lady on a pony; indirect lighting; etched-glass mirrors; murals of flamingos and bare-bosom'd Balinese beauties; leopard-skin banquettes; and a dining room with a real stream running through it that looks as if it had been designed by Paul Bunyan.

The Rendezvous

NEW HOTEL JEFFERSON · · · · · · SAINT LOUIS, MO.

4A-H1893

A fascinating change in taste is revealed in two cards showing the chic Rendezvous Lounge of the New Hotel Jefferson, "The Aristocrat of St. Louis," whose foreboding exterior is pictured on page 51. The original cheerful Art Deco color scheme from 1934 featured red and yel-

The Rendezvous

NEW HOTEL JEFFERSON · · · · SAINT LOUIS, MO.

low seating and a very smart Vitrolite and etched-mirror bar. By 1945, the bar had been covered with dark wood and tufted leatherette, and the color scheme was much more sober. (The later view is from the opposite end of the room.)

88

THE BALINESE ROOM
Blackstone Hotel ~ Chicago
Containing the only Copper Dance Floor in America. Entertainment and music for dancing nightly. Serving luncheon, dinner and supper.

CHICAGO
MAR 13

BALINESE ROOM — THE BLACKSTONE HOTEL — CHICAGO

The BILTMORE
MADISON AVE. AT 43RD STREET, NEW YORK

Royal Palm Roof — The Biltmore — New York City

89

THE FIFE & DRUM
HOTEL WITHERILL
Plattsburg, N. Y.

Restaurant and Bar located in the Witherill Hotel serves Fine Food and Beverages at popular prices and is considered one of America's outstanding rooms.

THE
FIFE & DRUM

90

With its unrivalled location on beautiful Copley Square lending a charm of historic atmosphere. THE COPLEY PLAZA imparts to its guest through the quality of its appointments, a cherished welcome. Truly, luxurious refinement without extravagance.

THE COPLEY PLAZA   **BOSTON, MASS.**
CHAUNCEY DEPEW STEELE, MANAGER

Hotel George Washington
★ ★ ★ ★ "23" ROOM ★ ★ ★ ★
A new Ultra Modern Cocktail Lounge
Never A Cover Or Minimum Charge
Continuous Entertainment
23 Lexington Ave.   Cor. 23rd St.
Open 2 P.M. to 3 A.M.

HOTEL GEORGE WASHINGTON "23" ROOM

91

MERRY-GO-ROUND BAR — RITZ-CARLTON HOTEL — ATLANTIC CITY, NEW JERSEY

6A-H810

FAMOUS MERRY-GO-ROUND
"Scientifically Air-Conditioned"
RITZ-CARLTON HOTEL
ATLANTIC CITY
The Boardwalk's most unique rendezvous, where there
is dancing daily at cocktail hour, dinner and supper,
the year 'round.

McCOLGAN HOTEL CAFE — McCOMB, MISS.

AIR-CONDITIONED

8A-H1326

McCOLGAN HOTEL and CAFE
Air-Conditioned, Located on U. S. Highway 51
McCOMB, MISSISSIPPI
Best town, hotel and cafe in South Mississippi.
XAVIER A. KRAMER, President
OFFICIAL AAA HOTEL

92

YMCA HOTEL
826 S. Wabash Avenue — CHICAGO
● For Men, Women and Families. 2000 Fireproof rooms.
Many with running water. Some with private bath.
Rates from 75¢ to $2.50 per day. Three floors reserved
for women and families. Large lobbies and lounges.
Daily programs, entertainments and concerts Restau-
rants, Barber Shop, Tailor Shop, Haberdashery, Travel
Bureau, Health Club.

THE CAFETERIA — YMCA HOTEL — CHICAGO

3A-H629

COFFEE SHOP — SKIRVIN HOTEL — OKLAHOMA CITY, OKLA.

6A-H67

THE SKIRVIN HOTEL COFFEE SHOP on the lobby floor of the Skirvin Hotel, Oklahoma City, Okla. is one of the largest and most beautiful in the Southwest. Architecture, fixtures and decorations are modernistic in detail and both ceiling and walls are acoustically treated to reduce noise to a minimum. The room is iced air cooled in Summer.

Of course, we need a little reality, too, so here are a few coffee shops with reassuring tile floors, booths, or counters where we can start our day with eggs over easy and white toast with jelly, and where we can write those post cards to the kids and Aunt Ida, who's home looking after them, just to let them know we're thinking of them and wish they were here.

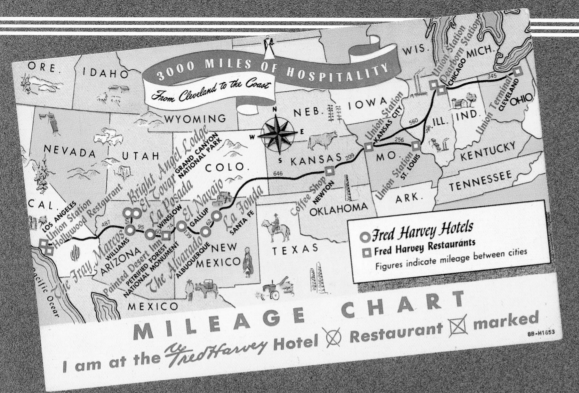

his book would not have happened without the help of several people, and I would like to express my thanks to them here: to Russell McDougal, Cha Cha Hertz, Merle Peek, Gloria Elissha, and Bob Carlson, who schlepped to antique show after antique show while I was filling out the nucleus of the collection of cards that grew into this album (not that they minded it one bit!); to Susan Mitchell, whose encouragement and suggestions helped produce a far more varied and interesting design; to Michele Weisman, whose interest led me to Erica Marcus, my editor, whose enthusiasm and bright humor helped turn a personal collection into a book to be shared; to my produc-

tion editor, Mark McCauslin, who helped prevent my sentences from running on into the next state; to Ceil Singer, Sy Lemler, and the type wizards at Typographic Images, Inc.; to the many post card dealers who sent me packets of cards that so enriched the original collection; to Katherine Hamilton-Smith and Debra Gust of the Curt Teich Postcard Archives at the Lake County Museum, who provided much of the factual material about Curt Teich & Company; and most of all, to the countless anonymous photographers, retouch artists, printers, and business people whose combined efforts created the cards this book is intended to honor.

ACKNOWLEDGMENTS

129—A GUEST ROOM, LA FONDA HOTEL, SANTA FE, N. M.
The unique decorations and furnishings in La Fonda are a rare combination of the Old World and the New. Brilliant Indian and Mexican colors and designs are blended into a delightful and cheerful whole.
PHOTO COURTESY FRED HARVEY CO.

here are more than sixty post card clubs in the United States and Canada, most of which have monthly meetings where members can buy and sell cards and admire one another's collections. Most publish newsletters.

An invaluable source of information on post card clubs, history, sales, shows, auctions, and various local activities is *Postcard Collector* magazine. Its classified advertising section is particularly useful. Subscriptions are $17.95 for 12 monthly issues and are available from Joe Jones Publishing, P.O. Box 337, Iola, WI 54945 (Telephone: 715 445-5000).

The Curt Teich Postcard Archives at the Lake County Museum, which is a department of the Lake County Forest Preserve, is located about forty miles northwest of Chicago. It is devoted to the preservation, exhibition, and interpretation of the archives of Curt Teich & Company of Chicago, which produced most of the cards in this book. Membership categories and dues are as follows: individual, $15; family/group, $20; institutional nonprofit, $20; contributing, $35; sustaining, $150; life (one-time payment), $500. Membership includes a subscription to the attractive and informative illustrated quarterly publication, *Image File*. Dues and inquiries should be addressed to the Curt Teich Archives, Lake County Museum, Lakewood Forest Preserve, Wauconda, IL 60084 (Telephone: 708 526-8638).

RESOURCES

50   ELEPHANT HOTEL, MARGATE CITY, AN OLD LANDMARK, ATLANTIC CITY, N. J.

THE ONLY ELEPHANT IN THE WORLD YOU CAN GO THROUGH AND COME OUT ALIVE

3A-H1206

This famous building erected in 1885 was
one of what was to be a menagerie of such
hotels.   The elephant   contains   ten   rooms
and is visited by thousands.

HOTEL SENATE

467 Turk St. at Larkin -- SAN FRANCISCO, CALIF.

Just two short blocks from CIVIC CENTER, where new
Federal, State, Municipal and Western Furniture Exchange
Buildings are located.

Rooms with Bath and Shower
Single $1.50, $1.75 and $2.00 . . . . Double $2.00, $2.25 and $2.50

Rooms with Detached Bath and Shower
Single $1.00 and $1.25 . . . . Double $1.50 and $1.75

Rooms with Bath and Shower -- 2 Double Beds
3 Persons . . . . $3.00   4 Persons $4.00

Hotel el-Rancho

GALLUP, NEW MEXICO
TURNER TOURIST HOTELS INC.

On U. S. Hi-Way "66"

A Commercial Hotel -- A Tourist Rendezvous

● New and modern -- architecturally interest-
ing with many unusual features -- Terrace,
Patio, Cowboy Bunks for Children, Sleeping
Porches, Cocktail Lounge and Bar, Coffee
Shop, Dining Room.

Accommodations for 250 Guests
Rates Surprisingly Low

"Come as you Are"

EAT AND SLEEP IN A WIGWAM

A novel, unique and modern motor court
that offers an atmosphere of comfort, clean-
liness and refinement. A tile bath, radio,
ceiling fan and heater for each Sleeping
Wigwam. All furniture of rustic, solid hickory
wood. Located within city limits. Fireproof.

Hotel Mayfair

POST CARD

ATLANTIC TOWERS HOTEL

at 4201 Collins Avenue   MIAMI BEACH, FLORIDA

On the Ocean

Private Beach — Cocktail Lounge — Dining
Room — Solarium — Elevator Service
Garden — Parking Facilities

THE BOWMAN HOTEL

220—23rd Street ∴ Miami Beach, Florida

Ideally located across the street from Roney Plaza and Row-
man Pools. One block from bathing beach, pools and golf
course . . One hundred outside rooms with combination
tub and shower bath . . Solarium for women and men on
roof . . A new and in every way an up-to-the-minute
hotel . . Convenient to all events of importance.

Regards from the Sunny South.

THIS SPACE FOR WRITING MESSAGES

Hello Pal:
I sure am having a
swell time I wish
you were here to go
swimming with us
tonight! Luther and

POST CARD

THIS SPACE FOR ADDRESS ONLY